Rooster's Off to See the World

ERIC CARLE

 Glenview, Illinois • Boston, Massachusetts • Chandler, Arizona • Upper Saddle River, New Jersey

Copyright © 1972 by Eric. Carle. All rights reserved.

Little Book version of *Rooster's Off to See the World* is published by Pearson.

All rights reserved. Printed in the United States of America. This publication is protected by copyright, and permission should be obtained from the publisher prior to any prohibited reproduction, storage in a retrieval system, or transmission in any form or by any means, electronic, mechanical, photocopying, recording, or likewise. For information regarding permissions, write to Pearson Curriculum Rights & Permissions, One Lake Street, Upper Saddle River, New Jersey 07458.

Pearson® is a trademark, in the U.S. and/or in other countries, of Pearson plc or its affiliates.
Scott Foresman® is a trademark, in the U.S and/or in other countries, of Pearson Education, Inc., or its affiliates.

ISBN 13: 978-0-328-47239-0
ISBN 10:   0-328-47239-5

12 13 14 15 V010 18 17 16 15

One fine morning, a rooster decided that he wanted to travel.
So, right then and there, he set out to see the world.
He hadn't walked very far when he began to feel lonely.

Just then, he met two cats. The rooster said to them, "Come along with me to see the world." The cats liked the idea of a trip very much. "We would love to," they purred and set off down the road with the rooster.

As they wandered on, the rooster and the cats met three frogs. "How would you like to come with us to see the world?" asked the rooster, eager for more company.
"Why not?" answered the frogs.
"We are not busy now." So the frogs jumped along behind the rooster and the cats.

After a while, the rooster, the cats, and the frogs saw four turtles crawling slowly down the road.
"Hey," said the rooster, "how would you like to see the world?"
"It might be fun," snapped one of the turtles and they joined the others.

9

As the rooster, the cats, the frogs, and the turtles walked along, they came to five fish swimming in the brook.
"Where are you going?" asked the fish.
"We're off to see the world," answered the rooster.
"May we come along?" pleaded the fish.
"Delighted to have you," the rooster replied.
And so the fish came along to see the world.

The sun went down. It began to get dark. The moon came up over the horizon. "Where's our dinner?" asked the cats. "Where are we supposed to sleep?" asked the frogs. "We're cold," complained the turtles.

Just then, some fireflies flew overhead. "We're afraid," cried the fish. Now, the rooster really had not made any plans for the trip around the world. He had not remembered to think about food and shelter, so he didn't know how to answer his friends.

After a few minutes of silence, the fish suddenly decided that it might be best if they headed for home. They wished the others a happy trip and swam away.

Then, the turtles began to think about their warm house. They turned and crawled back down the road without so much as a good-bye.

The frogs weren't too happy with the trip anymore, either. First one and then the other and finally the last one jumped away. They were polite enough, though, to wish the rooster a good evening as they disappeared into the night.

The cats then remembered an unfinished meal they had left behind. They kindly wished the rooster a happy journey and they, too, headed for home.

Now the rooster was all alone – and he hadn't seen anything of the world. He thought for a minute and then said to the moon, "To tell you the truth, I am not only hungry and cold, but I'm homesick as well."
The moon did not answer. It, too, disappeared.

The rooster knew what he had to do.
He turned around and went back home again.
He enjoyed a good meal of grain and then sat
on his very own perch.

After a while he went to sleep and had a wonderful happy dream – all about a trip around the world!